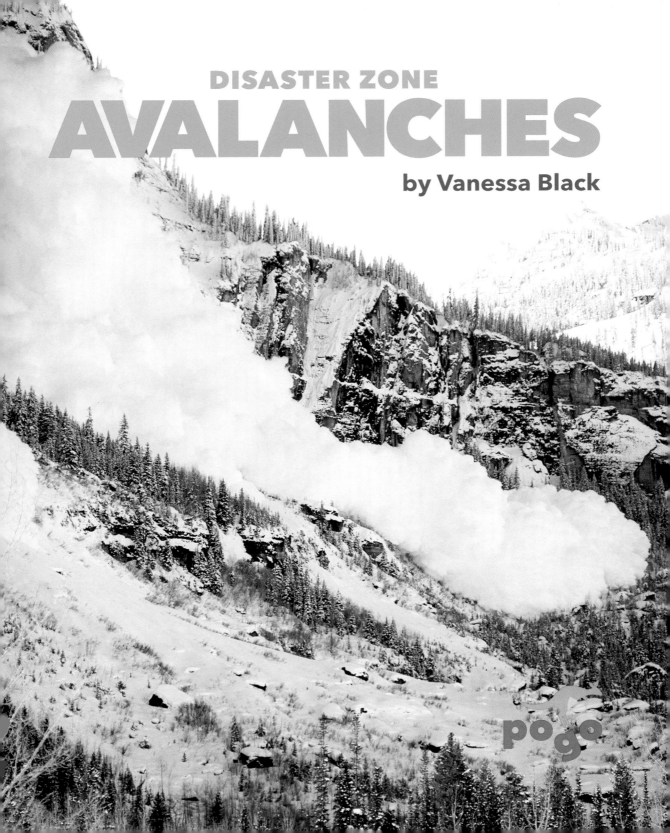

DISASTER ZONE
AVALANCHES

by Vanessa Black

pogo

Ideas for Parents and Teachers

Pogo Books let children practice reading informational text while introducing them to nonfiction features such as headings, labels, sidebars, maps, and diagrams, as well as a table of contents, glossary, and index.

Carefully leveled text with a strong photo match offers early fluent readers the support they need to succeed.

Before Reading

- "Walk" through the book and point out the various nonfiction features. Ask the student what purpose each feature serves.
- Look at the glossary together. Read and discuss the words.

Read the Book

- Have the child read the book independently.
- Invite him or her to list questions that arise from reading.

After Reading

- Discuss the child's questions. Talk about how he or she might find answers to those questions.
- Prompt the child to think more. Ask: Have you ever been somewhere an avalanche might occur?

Pogo Books are published by Jump!
5357 Penn Avenue South
Minneapolis, MN 55419
www.jumplibrary.com

Library of Congress Cataloging-in-Publication Data

Names: Black, Vanessa, author.
Title: Avalanches / by Vanessa Black.
Description: Minneapolis, MN: Jump!, Inc., [2016] Series: Disaster zone | "Pogo Books are published by Jump!"
Audience: Ages 7-10. | Includes bibliographical references and index.
Identifiers: LCCN 2016028286 (print)
LCCN 2016029216 (ebook)
ISBN 9781620315637 (hardcover: alk. paper)
ISBN 9781620316030 (pbk.)
ISBN 9781624965111 (ebook)
Subjects: LCSH: Avalanches—Juvenile literature.
Classification: LCC QC929.A8 B527 2016 (print)
LCC QC929.A8 (ebook) | DDC 551.57/848—dc23
LC record available at https://lccn.loc.gov/2016028286

Editor: Kirsten Chang
Series Designer: Anna Peterson
Book Designer: Leah Sanders
Photo Researchers: Kirsten Chang and Leah Sanders

Photo Credits: Adobe Stock, 6-7; Alamy, 18-19, 20-21; Getty, 10-11, 13, 14-15; iStock, cover, 1, 5; National Geographic Creative, 12; Shutterstock, 3, 4, 16, 17, 23; Superstock, 8-9.

Printed in the United States of America at Corporate Graphics in North Mankato, Minnesota.

TABLE OF CONTENTS

CHAPTER 1

IT'S AN AVALANCHE!

You are driving on a mountain road. Look! Up ahead! Snow is sliding down the mountain. You pull over and watch.

The snow picks up speed. It rushes toward the road. It's an avalanche!

Luckily, it's a small one. Drivers saw it. They were able to stop. No one was hurt. However, you are stuck. There is a big pile of snow and **debris** on the road. You have to wait for a plow.

DID YOU KNOW?

In about five seconds, a slide can reach speeds of 80 miles (129 kilometers) per hour.

Avalanches happen when **snowpack** becomes unstable and breaks off. Many things can **trigger** them. Earthquakes, warm weather, and wind are triggers. Sometimes skiers and hikers cause slides. Sometimes they are big slides. Sometimes they are small.

DID YOU KNOW?

Loose snow avalanches are called sluffs.

Slab avalanches are very dangerous. They happen when a hard layer of snow sits on top of a weak, soft layer. The soft layer cannot support the heavy hard layer. It breaks off. The slab slides. As it slides, it picks up snow, rocks, and trees. It can move up to 200 miles (322 km) per hour!

TAKE A LOOK!

What does an avalanche look like?

☐ = strong slab
☐ = weak, loose layer
■ = packed snow
■ = mountain

CHAPTER 2

DEADLY AVALANCHES

In 1970, an earthquake caused part of a **glacier** to collapse in **Peru**. The result was deadly.

glacier

Giant chunks of ice fell. They slid down the mountain. As they slid, they picked up mud and rocks. Two towns were buried, and 20,000 people died.

From 1950 to 1951 there were more than 600 avalanches in Europe. More than 265 people died over three months. It was known as the Winter of Terror.

WHERE DO THEY HAPPEN?

Most avalanches occur in snowy, mountainous regions.

■ = Avalanche-Prone Areas

CHAPTER 3

STAYING SAFE

How can you stay safe? Do not go in areas that are prone to slides.

AVALANCHES

Never explore mountains alone.

If you are playing in the mountain snow, always have safety gear. A **beacon** sends out signals if you are buried. Use a shovel to dig out others. A **probe** pokes in the snow to look for buried people.

probe

beacon

If you see a slide, get out of the way! Move to the side, and grab a tree. If you get caught in it, make swimming motions to stay on top. If you are buried, dig an air pocket around your mouth. Then, spit. That will tell you which way is up.

Be prepared, and you can stay safe in an avalanche.

DID YOU KNOW?

Dogs are trained to find buried people. One can search 2½ acres (1 hectare) in 30 minutes. It takes 20 people about four hours to cover that same area.

MAKE AN AVALANCHE

Does loose snow affect how avalanches form? Try this simple activity and find out.

What You Need:
- two heavy books
- salt

1. **Put one book on the floor. This represents the ground.**

2. **Put the second book on top of the first book. This represents snowpack.**

3. **Gently raise one side of the first book until the second book slides.**

4. **Replace the first book on the floor.**

5. **Sprinkle salt on top of the book.**

6. **Place the second book on top of the salt. This represents loose snow.**

7. **Gently raise the first book again and watch the second book slide. What changes? Does the "avalanche" happen slower or faster when salt is added? Why do you think this happens?**

beacon: A piece of gear that sends out a radio signal.

debris: Things, like rocks and sticks, that are left after a disaster.

glacier: A large, thick ice mass.

Peru: A country in South America.

probe: A long stick used for sticking in the snow to locate buried people.

snowpack: A mass of snow that is built up over time and often compressed.

trigger: Something that sets something else off.

INDEX

TO LEARN MORE

Learning more is as easy as 1, 2, 3.

1) Go to www.factsurfer.com

2) Enter "avalanches" into the search box.

3) Click the "Surf" button to see a list of websites.

With factsurfer, finding more information is just a click away.